I0141611

THE LIFE DIALOGUE

LD

my Breasts TALKING

And I finally decided to listen!

KARRIE ROSS

My Breasts Talking™
And I finally decided to listen!
Karrie Ross

www.MyBreastsTalking.com

All rights reserved
Copyright © 2011 Be It Now!, Karrie Ross

A Be-It-Now! Book

All rights reserved. No part of this book may be reproduced or transmitted in any form or by any means, electronic or mechanical, including photocopying, recording or by any other information storage and retrieval system, without written permission from the author. My Breasts Talking™ and Be It Now!®, are registered trademarks. By buying and reading this book you agree to the following: You understand that this is simply a set of opinions (and not advice) based on the author's experience. You are responsible for your own well-being, and hold Be It Now!, Karrie Ross. and all members and affiliates harmless in any claim or event resulting from your reading, use or application of the viewpoints shared in the book.

Printed in the United States of America

Book Design: www.KarrieRoss.com
My Breasts Talking illustrations are
©2011 Karrie Ross All rights reserved.

Books are available for special promotions,
large quantity book sales, and premiums.
For details contact:
Published by Be It Now!® Los Angeles, CA 90066
books@beitnow.com

ISBN 13: 978-0-9723366-5-9 Paperback

Disclaimer: This book is not for the victims of the world who want to blame others for their problems. Some of the observations may be X-rated. The ideas presented are based on the author's experience and contributions from others. Your choice to read, consider or use the information is your own. And you take responsibility for yourself and your emotional well-being.

To *The Girls* everywhere.
Long may we thrive.

Spiral Series: Bustiers:
"Love Is All There Is!"
2011

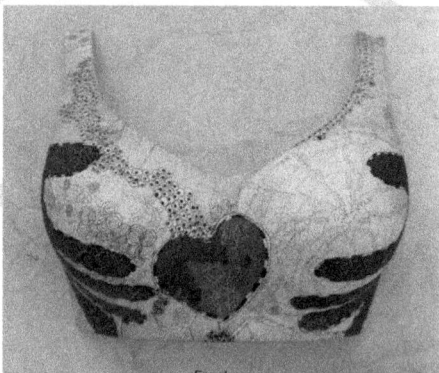

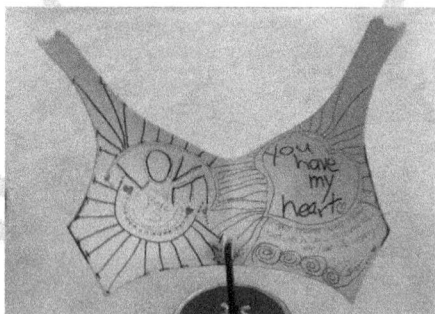

Why?

If your body could speak, what would it say?

This all started when I was considering what to paint next and I decided to apply my Spiral Series look to a plastic bra form. As I began painting and drawing on the form, the front, of course, was where I put all my attention and creativity. I was happily on my way to finishing off the fourth one. When I turned it around to sign it, like I'd done the three previous ones, the aha of the blank back caused me to question what I could put there. After long consideration, I arrived at the realization that "the front is what I show to the world and the back reflects my internal thoughts."

WOW! and the rest is history.

If there were one feature that stands out as being there and affecting my life, it would have to be my breasts. Sure my eyes, ears, nose, mouth, arms, hands, legs, feet, head, heart, butt, knees etc. have all been here too. But for me, my breasts, being right out in front and getting lots of attention, caused the most discomfort, and I truly don't know when it began. Maybe that is why I assigned a personality to them and they began talking (yes, I know it's just me talking to me). Or maybe that happened because I am connected to and observe how my body exists...or it could just be an extention of my expression as an artist giving voice to an inner wisdom.

I believe the best way to create a happy healthy self is to attend to the internal dialogue that is going on within us all the time, the act of observing and listening to what is being said, attending to and assessing those unique conversations. Yes, I said conversations...you do talk to yourself, don't you? I'm seldom alone.

I'm not writing this book to bring attention to my breasts. My intention is to address the issues of having and living with them—their uniqueness and idiosyncracies. I realize that for every female or male out there, there are a set of breasts with a different viewpoint, based on a different set of life experiences.

Some choose to get implants or reductions. Others choose to show them off or hide them. Choices. And each set of breasts has a unique voice and some-thing special to share if you're listening.

My Breasts Talking is about my breasts' observa-tions and the interesting conversations we have. They are expressive and definitely have a voice that is unique... you know, one that stands out from the rest of the body.

I've been listening to them *talking* for a long time now and I've finally decided that we need to share our thoughts and observations.

We've had a long life. We've been through the teens, wearing a bra and not wearing a bra, first sex, more sex, pregnancy, motherhood, nursing, child-raising, gaining and losing weight, exercise, getting older, clothing trends, and more that we'll share with you throughout the book.

There will be a mix of emotions and perspectives. Funny. Happy. Serious. Humorous. Physical. Sexy. Strange. Shocking. Bouncing. Positive/Negative. Other people's viewpoints.

The dialogue will be coming from both me and my breasts and others who have contributed. When "I" speak, (which didn't happen often) it reflects my inner dialogue or self talk. When "we" speak, my breasts are sharing their sentiments. They are like a precocious two-year-old talking, talking, talking... wanting attention, complaining, giving orders... expressing!

What is your internal conversation saying?

_____

_____

_____

_____

_____

_____

Q.

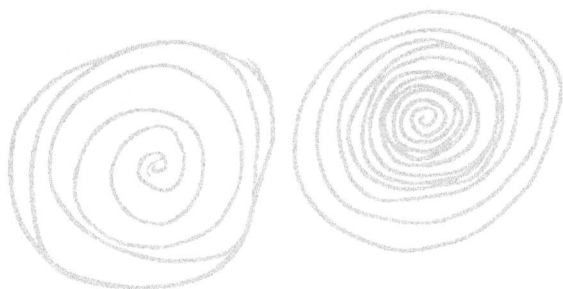

If your BREASTs had a voice, what is the **one thing** they would want to say?

my
Breasts
TALKING

The Girls

The first time I heard that phrase I wondered what they were talking about. Then I realized a few seconds later, "It's my breasts!" They were talking about my breasts.

WOW! Now we have a reference name other than breasts, boobies, teats.

If love makes the world go round, we will do ourselves well to acknowledge the impact breasts have on the world. They play a big part in populating the planet, and they supply the first food for most humans. Breasts help to provide a sense of comfort, security and give life from love.

Breast envy...
Why?

"You can't walk away from your truth."

We are breasts and we are included with each body. We are not created equal. We may differ by our size, shape, color and internal make-up but we are still breasts and...

It feels good just to say that.

We really like being in water, naked... we float! Takes the weight off the shoulders.

My Breasts Talking

What are you looking at? Haven't you ever seen breasts before?

Step away from the breasts

...if you know what's good for you!

Stop looking at us when you're talking.

Eyes Up!

Look at her face, her eyes, her mouth...

please!

Who designed bras anyway? We don't think they ever had to wear one...they feel like a harness!

Training bra, or that is what they called it. What the heck was it training? We weren't even looking like breasts yet. We were only nipples.

It did have a pretty flower though, right in the middle…but geez, when we wore a sweater, it looked like we were three nipples.

WHAT were they thinking?

Must have been designed by a man.

Are there any breasts that look like us?

We finally found some when we went to the Playboy photography studio... There on the wall was a photo display of all the previous centerfold models... and there were two whose areolae looked like ours... Yay!

We really like the new empire waist tops…love the v-neck that shows off our cleavage. But whoever designs them has no concept of where breasts hang from small to large or young to old.

For us, the usual location for where the empire waist is placed cuts us off in the middle, right at our nipple!

What the heck?

When I look down I can't see my feet...

My breasts are all I see!

We know the doctor said to breast feed for longer than 6 months, but we hurt.

Have you seen some of the push-up bras... just where do they think we're going?

My Breasts Talking

We had a man once tell us that we were our body's best asset!

...that conversation didn't last long.

We loved not having to wear a bra and didn't for many years...

the younger years!

What! We're pregnant! Wow! We're going to grow and grow and get bigger all the time...bigger, bigger bigger....

Ouch! Now we're sore too...!

Oh! He touched us. He held us in his hands and snuggled in. Wow... that is a first. We kinda like that ...ooooo we are getting excited... and he can tell.

We are not big fans of lying face down, especially when we are tender from menstruation. We were not really happy with that.

We are not the same size, you know. Our left one is bigger than the right one...kinda like with feet!

We know running is good exercise but when you are as big as we are, the bouncing gets to be a little out-of-hand and sports bras leave a lot to be desired.

No wonder the eyes look at us so much!

Naked!
Oh we like this...

NAKED!

When we wear a bra with a plastic front closing, it sometimes pops if we are squeezed together...really.

We are forever amazed at the big fuss that is made over us...

Being big has its benefits... sexually, really. More to play with in so many different ways! oh my...

Torpedo breasts.

What, you've never seen a movie made in the 1950s /1960s? The breasts that sit way high and are pointy!

Well, after wearing the bra all day, the breasts become "molded" to the shape.

When I first noticed it, I laughed so hard... and then immediately started looking for a new bra with a differnt cup shape.

Safety pins unite... they have saved many a blouse with the peek-a-boo openings.

We always have one with us.

Toilet paper, cotton and tissues were a must for any training bra, especially when nipples were all we were and the bra wasn't padded. The boys would point and make fun of us. It was better to stuff the bra with something to hide the protruding nipples.

We knew some bras that were stuffed for the longest time...

Cold!

US?

How can you tell?

Shelf-bra cami top.

For some very strange reason, that just doesn't sound right to us!

Breasts

Boobs

Boobies

Boobettes

Tits

Teats

Titties

Bosom

The Girls

Ladies

The thinking behind bra sizing:

Training Bra = our nipples no longer are flat

AA = our areolae have a little mound behind them

A = just to make us feel like we're growing

B = we are full, firm, perky

C = we really are getting attention

D = oh my goodness, we bounce all the time

DD = isn't there any bra that can hold us?

E = ok...who designed these straps?

EE = eeks!

F = @#(!>*#%^$*!$

In the way...!

In the way of what?

What are we stopping you from doing by being on your chest?

So what if we are rather large....

We're told we look great with diamonds!

My Breasts Talking

We have a life of our own...

are you interested?

Caress us. See how we respond. We love to turn men on....Who says it's not easy?

Cleavage.

Need I say more?

Picture this.

Woman wearing low cut top.
Woman bending over.
Breasts fall out.

Are you laughing?
Then it hasn't happened to you.

Jumping jacks make us hurt without the proper bra for support.

We think our size makes it difficult to do some yoga positions.

We're sure it's all about balance!

Aren't all breasts able to be excited?

Personally, I'd be more concerned about what's going on in the mind.

Crumb catcher or shelf are two other names, especially for larger breasts, that really stick out and seem to be able to catch food that falls.

pointy

jutting

protruding

soft

bouncy

perky

flat

hard

implants

falsies

saggy

The way this date is going, he's going to be lucky to even touch us!

Hugs.

    Close hugs.

We like close hugs.

Squishy yes... but we only squish so much!

Good posture can make or break us.

We are friends. We feel the same joy and pain, seen as equal except in size.

We feel and sense. We love to be seen and held and caressed... and respected for our responsiveness when we are.

We might seem like inanimate objects... but we're not. We respond.

We remember that breast health is important and our doctor reminds us each year.

But that doesn't mean we like being squished in that machine!

Still, after all these years, we haven't gotten use to wearing a bra... which for our size is mandatory... Maybe we never will.

Too confining.

Perky. Saggy.
We are what we are.

Cami tops...watch out for our nipples...if you don't pay attention to how we are placed, it might make us seem lopsided!

We haven't done anything wrong. Don't get a breast reduction... please. We'll be good.

Bigger is not necessarily better... or smaller not necessarily worse.

We were hippie breasts.

Don't ask.

Naked!

Oops! I think I said that already.

We are the voice of motherhood!   (59)

Why is it that the AA size cup is smaller than an A, but the DD size cup is larger than D?

There was a time when the only comfortable bra we could find had a little padding for shape and to lessen the nipple presence.

Hello..! size 36C doesn't need any of that.

For years, a certain retail bra catalogue was a lifesaver for us. So many really pretty bras and all with an easy-to-fasten front closing.

Then they changed and started offering only one front closure. But it only comes with elastic straps!

Hello...! Bouncy bouncy already an issue, we don't need more elastic... or at least not the full strap!

What happens in a bra...
stays in a bra!

My Breasts Talking

In gym class we learned an exercise that was supposed to keep us perky...ready?

All together now....

    1. elbows out

    2. palms together

    3. now push

And the resulting action was... we bounced!

WAY soooo funny to watch!

There was a verse that went with this...

"We must. We must. We must improve our bust."

We've found that men really like to pay attention to us, to fondle us and to kiss us.

We wonder if they hear us talking.

We are the voice of femininity!

We can really feel how heavy we are when she takes off the bra!

Who was it that said she wasn't carrying the weight of the world on her shoulders?

Bathing suits...we like the ones that sell the two pieces separately.

And we like the ones that have at least one of those cami shelf-bra type inserts or a bra closure to help us stay up.

We are not keen on the ones that just let us hang in there...

...if we can!

How we breasts fall...

When she lies on her back, we fall to the sides.

When she lies on her side, we flatten off on top of each other.

And when she leans over, we're just kinda left hanging there.

We remember the good olde days...

But why dwell on what was?
We only have today.

We are soft, and we like to be held...snuggled... but not squeezed.

The bra we wear has an underwire...

We don't know why the wire is there, it doesn't seem to help!

Are we missing something...?

Bouncy, Bouncy!

So maybe,

if we can't always get what we want...

we can be happy as long as we get what we need.

We are happy! [smile]

Dancing...

WooHoo!

A meeting of two minds.

What are yours saying?

Are you ready...

quickly now...

Shift and adjust!

There were times in our lives when we wanted to yell... "What the heck is happening to us???" It seems that being pregnant and getting older were two things we hadn't counted on changing us so much...

We just hate it when we get an itch near the nipple, it's almost impossible to scratch it without being seen!

Why is it that when our body needs to get through a narrow space, the stomach can be pulled in...

but we can't!

Have a GREAT Breasts Day!

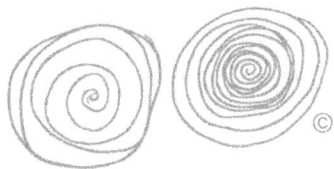

We are the voice of nurture...

Sticky...oh so sticky when it's hot...

Breast pump?

We do not think this was any help at all. It seemed as though the more milk we pumped out, the *way* more we made!

When we were pregnant and went to the beach, our body's hands would dig holes in the sand for us and the large belly.

What a sight we were...!

Peek-a-boo! We just love poking out of these fun flaps on nursing bras.

If men had bigger breasts...

...would they like those darn seat belt straps

...would they still want to firmly squeeze us

...would they like to wear a bra

...could they handle the distractions

then we might....

We once saw an ad for a bra insert that makes it look like our nipples are always erect?

Whatever happened to looking natural?

We either are or aren't...Remember, not all breasts are created the same,

and,

we love the way we are!

Contributor Stories

When my younger sister's breasts got bigger before mine, I told her it was just "fat".

(contributor story)

The bra is the most overrated piece of clothing next to a tight pair of jeans.

(contributor story)

My Breasts Talking

When I get to heaven, I'm going to give the person who invented the bra a piece of my mind.

(contributor story)

I've been known to unhook my bra while driving out of the parking lot after a long day at the office.

(contributor story)

They used to be perky. Now they're going south.

(contributor story)

They're just mammary glands, Get over it!

(contributor story)

A friend of mine who was very small breasted had a t-shirt with very small print that said "little teats," "little teats" all over it.

(contributor story)

Some Hollywood award shows should be renamed "Teaty City."

(contributor story)

How dumb was it to write in my diary about the first time a boy removed my bra? Especially when I had one of those moms who felt it was her job to invade my privacy.

(contributor story)

I can remember seeing my mom bending over to put her bra on...to make sure her boobs filled the cups properly. As a teenager it was "gross," as a woman now in my 60s, it was good training!

(contributor story)

I never really thought much about my boobs (they were always boobs to me) when I was growing up....actually, let me take that back. When I was in about the 3rd grade, I was dusting a bookshelf at home and there were some small, cup-like dessert dishes kept there. I put two of them over my non-existent boobs, which made them kind of "swell up" under the glass cups! I think my Mom walked in and asked, "What are you doing?" and I was mortified but denied the obvious. "Just dusting....."

(contributor story)

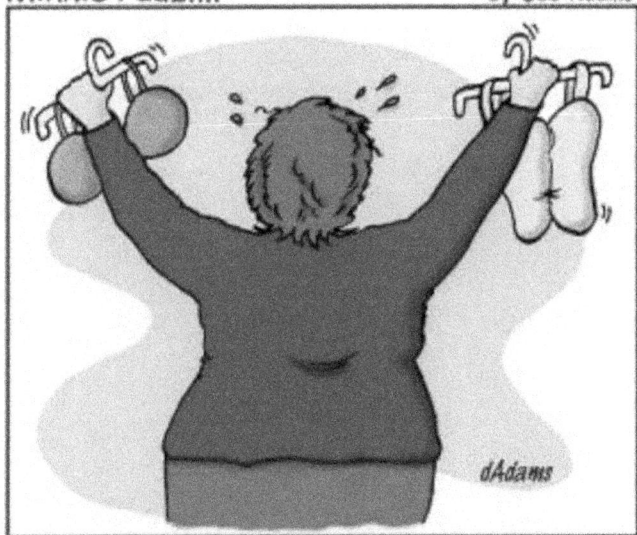

Minnie Pauz....™   by Dee Adams

Lord, when did I go from a 36D to a 36 LONG???

(contributor story)

Push-up bras = false advertising.

(contributor story)

I remember the first time I felt my breasts jiggle. I was running across the street and I thought, Wow! A revelation for a 14-year-old.

(contributor story)

In high school, I had a conversation with a friend about buying bras. We are both small-breasted and she was lamenting the stretchy "one-size fits all" didn't fit. It made me laugh.

(contributor story)

A major retail store lingerie department carried a bra that I loved. On one shopping trip, I couldn't find it and asked a saleswomen. She looked me up and down and said, "What do you need one for?" I was so angry and taken aback at her rudeness, I just walked out of the store. I was in my 20s. She was probably in her 50s.

(contributor story)

I've always been happy with having small breasts. So much easier to deal with … clothes always fit and I don't get stared at. Plus, depending on what I am wearing, I can go braless.

(contributor story)

A friend and her husband were vacationing with friends at Bass Lake. She had on her bathing suit as they were getting ready to go out on the lake. She was looking around for her sunglasses and reached to her head thinking they were sitting on top. Then her friend said, "They're in your *ample* cleavage." She had rested the frames over the center of her top. She laughed and says to us, "...well, with my 34A, 'A' must stand for *ample*."

It cracked me up. From now on, I am going to think of A cup bras as " *ample*."

(*contributor story*)

Geez. Who knew a wardrobe malfunction could cause such a fuss? It's as if they never saw a breast before!

(contributor story)

We LOVE those monthly breast self-exams you give us in the shower. Drawing those tender little circles lets us know that you love us and want to maintain our health as well as your own.

(contributor story)

Melons, tits, teats, boobies, bosoms, tatas, bazooms, headlights, hooters.

Why do you think there are so many ways to describe us?

Do men and women call us different names, and if so, why is that?

(contributor story)

Karrie Ross

110

Damn! We just HATE those revolving doors at the airport. We're so afraid that it's not just the luggage that will get left behind.

(contributor story)

OH NO! Here comes that cold hard plate. It's going to squash us again. We may hate the way a mammogram feels, but we love that it helps keep us intact and alive.

(contributor story)

What price beauty!

What's wrong with a little sag?

(contributor story)

Woo Hoo! This burlesque gig is fun. Who knew we could get so good at twirling tassels?

(contributor story)

When a man behaves stupidly, some people call him a "boob." We find that very insulting. Then again, bad guys are also described using terms for the male appendage.

(contributor story)

Remember when you were a kid learning geography and all the boys laughed at the name "Lake Titicaca?"

We are not amused.

(contributor story)

Nursing mothers have sustained life on this planet since the beginning. Except in cases of medical necessity, we think fancy formulas are overrated.

(contributor story)

What's up with those covered statues? Shame is in the eye of the beholder.

(contributor story)

If you're offended by mothers nursing in public, close your eyes or go away! Most of the world doesn't bat an eye.

(contributor story)

Karrie's Conclusions...

In the end, we are not alone. We have a consistent chatter going on inside all the time. I hear my internal chatter. I guess it's my creative nature that assigned personalities, well really, more like attitudes, to what is being said. I seem to be better equiped to handle the constant chatter this way.

In my life, I've assigned attitudes to a lot of things, my car for one...and I've noticed that I seem sensitive to the energy of inanimate objects. I know, it's just my way of dealing with things. But I have to tell you... my internal life is not dull and I don't get bored very often... and I love to have fun and play.

The benefits of this way of looking at things is that you might begin:

- Taking life less seriously. This may help control your reaction to stress.

- Having or creating conversations with yourself which could lead to a higher level of trust in your decisions.

- Being your own best friend. Giving comfort whenever you need it.

- Assessing and changing what the negative chatter is saying and causing you to do/be/say.

- Allowing yourself to better "see" who you are being, each and every moment.

Acknowledgments

My Breasts Talking was a long time in coming.

Big Hugs and Thank Yous for Everyone!

- to every friend who contributed either their support or written words
- and a very big hug to my son who supports my artistic explorations

Without you all,
this never could have happened.

About the Author

Karrie Ross is a creative explorer. She lives her life in a state of mindful awareness.

A native to Los Angeles, California, Ross has lived a creative life. Her love of life and art process transports her to this state of being and she intends to stay *tuned in* as long as she can, bringing interesting points of view to any who are open to the experience.

As a self-proclaimed "hippie who caught the end of the movement," Ross is on a journey to find what she looks like... "I would walk by reflections in windows and for a split second wonder who it was..." This is not to say she feels that she has totally seen or found herself, for her, life is a constant observation of being. Nevertheless, she is intent on sharing her unique visions of life and strategies for how to get along in the world. Ross see's herself as a work in progress...

as aren't we all?

Karrie Ross is a Los Angeles based fine artist, graphic designer, award winning author, certified life coach, NLP, feng shui practitioner and mother. She paints and writes to share her unique view of the world inside and out. She is currently producing a series of books based on and in conjunction with her fine art spiral series... "The Life Dialogue™".

Visit our website and join the fun

www.TheLifeDialogue.com
www.MyBreastsTalking.com

www.ingramcontent.com/pod-product-compliance
Lightning Source LLC
Chambersburg PA
CBHW031320040426
42443CB00005B/161